TWO LIVES:
FLORENCE NIGHTINGALE
AND
MARY SEACOLE

First published in 1993 by Bogle-L'Ouverture Press Ltd.
64 Gifford Street, Islington, London N1, England

Printed by The Cromwell Press, Melksham, Wiltshire
Typeset by Contour Typesetters, Southall, Middx.

Cover illustration and Victorian Kitchen by Turu Pomel.

Line drawing of Florence and Parthenope walking with their father
by Julia Smith.

Map of the Crimea by David C. Collins.

Other illustrations reproduced by courtesy of Coventry Local
Education Authority

The questions and glossary have been complied by Carmel Cameron.
Born in Kingston, Jamaica, Carmel's primary and secondary
education took place both in Jamaica and Battersea, London. She is
the mother of two children, a teacher and active voluntary worker in
the supplementary school movement.

Printed by The Cromwell Press,
Broughton Gifford, Melksham,
Wiltshire SN12 8PH

DEDICATION

For Jessica who conceived and nurtured the series
to fulfillment.

Crimea

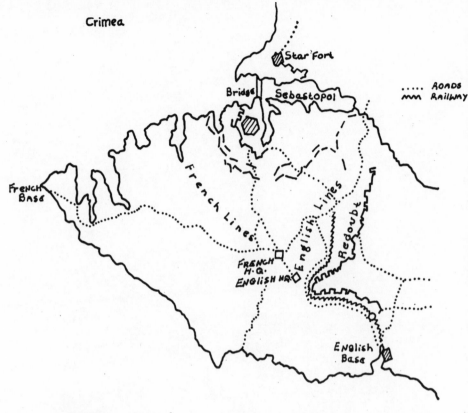

Star Fort

Bridge

Sebastopol

····· Roads
ᴖᴖ Railway

French Base

French Lines

English Lines

Redoubt

French H.Q.

English HQ.

English Base

Europe

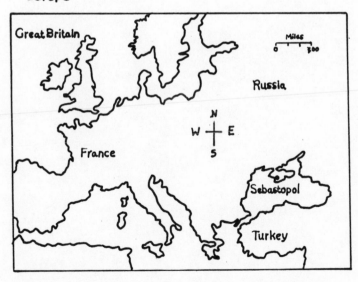

Great Britain

Russia

Miles
0   300

France

N
W ─┼─ E
S

Sebastopol

Turkey

FLORENCE NIGHTINGALE —
'THE WILD SWAN'

Florence As A Young Girl

CHAPTER 1

BIRTH

Florence Nightingale was born in the city of Florence in 1820. Her parents had fallen in love with the city which nestled along the banks of the River Arno in what is now Italy. Mr and Mrs Nightingale enjoyed its free atmosphere and the music for which the city was famous. When their second child was born, it seemed natural for them to name her after the city.

Florence's birth coincided with the end of a long series of wars in Europe. One of these wars came about as a result of the French emperor, Napoleon Bonaparte's attempt to set up a grand empire under French control. Napoleon fought nearly every country in Europe in his efforts to achieve his goal.

The end of these wars meant that people could travel again and countries could trade with each other as before. English people in those days used to travel on the continent of Europe. One was not considered to be a gentleman or lady unless one had visited the major European capitals. This was called the 'Grand Tour'. The Nightingales were one of those families who took advantage of the end of the wars to visit their favourite cities on a tour which lasted almost three years. They were able to afford this because they were very wealthy owners of large estates and lived in luxury and comfort.

In fact, it could be said that Florence was 'born with a silver spoon in her mouth'.

Florence, known as Flo, to her immediate family and close relatives and her sister, Parthe or Pop, short for Parthenope (she was born in Naples and named after one of the characters in the *Greek Myths*) were only a year apart in age, and as different as could be. Both shared some of their mother, Fanny's beauty, but it was Parthenope who took the fun and gaiety from their mother.

Florence was the more serious of the two and was tidy to a degree which caused many rows between the sisters. Parthenope was closer to her mother and took more to needlework, art, flower arranging and music than Florence. Florence on the other hand, was closer to her father. Both sisters were however excellent company for each other and enjoyed many activities together.

As was the custom among the wealthy, the two sisters were educated at home by tutors and their father. Parents felt that girls were to be prepared for a career of marriage, and that they only needed to learn music, needlework and the art of making intelligent conversation. However, Mr. Nightingale decided that he would become their tutor and keep them to a very strict routine wih a much broader range of subjects than would otherwise have been the case.

They were taught Latin, Greek, French, History, Mathematics and Literature. Florence, unlike Parthenope, found that History, Literature and Languages did not offer sufficient challenge and so turned more to Mathematics.

From an early age Florence was to display her independent spirit.
Even though she was well into her thirties before finally breaking
free. This line drawing by Florence's aunt, Julia Smith, is of
Florence, her father and sister Parthenope, out for a walk, and
was reproduced in the book, *Florence Nightingale*, written by
Mrs. Cecil Woodham Smith.

The Nightingales' had servants (footmen, gardeners,
maids, cooks and others) who looked after them and
their two houses. The girls were therefore left free of
housework. One of their houses was at Lea Hurst in
Derbyshire and had fifteen bedrooms but was considered too small. The summer months were spent
partly there while part of the autumn and winter were

spent at Elmsley Park near Romsey in Hampshire.

As both Florence's father and mother came from large families – Florence had at least twenty-four aunts and uncles not to mention countless cousins – their two homes had to be large enough and suitably located so as to enable them to entertain their family as well as their large circle of friends.

CHAPTER 2

CHILDHOOD

Both the houses in which Florence and Parthenope spent most of their childhood and youth were in grounds which resembled public parks. A specialist gardener was employed to landscape the grounds. Ponds and streams provided a natural habitat for geese, swans and ducks, while the new flowering plants and nursery attracted scores of multi-coloured flowers.

The sisters spent much of their spare time collecting butterflies and moths and playing in their secret tree house built among the boughs of low-lying trees. They also gave 'first aid' to their many cats, dogs and rabbits.

While Parthenope, her sister, loved to sketch, Florence preferred to write letters, notes and a daily diary – a pastime which remained a lifelong habit. The nineteenth century was the great age of letter writing. For Florence, the large number of aunts, uncles and cousins she had, together with the introduction of the Penny Post by Roland Hill in 1840, all combined to encourage her habit of writing.

Although her letter writing gave her some relief from the boredom she felt from time to time, she 'longed for some regular occupation, something worth doing, instead of frittering time away on useless trifles'. However, she did not stop at writing letters and she regularly wrote her thoughts on pieces of paper almost as though she were lonely with no one to talk to and therefore found it necessary to 'talk' to someone by writing down her thoughts. Later on in her life, she left specific instructions that her letters were to be destroyed after her death, many were nontheless preserved, and remain with us today providing a written record of her life and times.

Florence Begins To Take An Interest In The Poor

When the weather permitted, she would ride on her pony to the villages around her parents' estate. What she saw in these villages was to leave a deep impression on her. Although Florence had been used to daily contact with those villagers who were servants in her parents' houses, she was shocked to see the conditions in which they lived.

The tiny cottages, housing seven to ten people and the children dressed in little more than rags who lived and played in these hovels were all a sharp contrast to the finery, space and book-lined libraries of her parents' and their friends' houses. Florence shared what she dared with the villagers. Her soups, her time, tending to sick cats and dogs – all of these she gave freely and, when cholera struck, she helped nurse the young and old. Her parents disapproved strongly of her activities. Florence and Parthenope secretly taught their nursery maid, Bessie, to read and write.

Florence In Her Thirties

CHAPTER 3

FAMILY LIFE IN VICTORIAN TIMES

Trading With The Colonies

The income which made it possible for Florence and her family to live such a life of comfort came from both sides of the family. Most wealthy people invested in trade in Africa, the West Indies, the Americas and India. They bought and sold slaves, sugar, cotton, spices and other goods. These formed the source of wealth for many of these families, and the Nightingales were no exception. Their income also came from iron and coal mines.

However, both Florence's mother and father came from families with a strong tradition of supporting liberal causes. During the eighteenth and nineteenth centuries, there were a number of events and causes which many people felt very deeply about and which split opinions when people took one side or another.

Revolutionary Events in Florence's Family

Two of the events which caused deep divisions of opinion within Britain during the eighteenth century were the American War of Independence in 1775 and the French Revolution of 1789. In the nineteenth century, the century in which Florence was born as was Queen Victoria, some of the causes that were fought for concerned long-overdue reforms such as the Abolition of the Slave Trade in 1806. Other issues that had to be resolved were: how to provide cheaper food for the poor, how to give the vote to more people, how to free the millions of people enslaved in British colonies and how to improve the living and working conditions of the poor.

The 'Tories', later renamed 'Conservatives', clung to tradition and the 'old order', whilst the 'Whigs', later to be known as 'Liberals', represented the many factory owners and expanding middle classes who generally supported change and reform.

The Nightingales came from a tradition of support for the Whig cause; Florence's grandfather supported the Americans in their fight for independence from Britain. This was a brave act on his part and must have made him unpopular among Tories who were landowners like himself.

Florence's father supported efforts for improving the conditions of women and children in factories many of whom worked a twelve hour shift. He defended the rights of those who were not members of the Anglican Church to worship as they wished. He also founded a free school for the children of workers on his estate. Many of the visitors to the Nightingale household were the leading reformists of the day such as William Wilberforce and William Gladstone. So, when in 1834 Mr. Nightingale was chosen to stand for Parliament as a Whig MP, the entire family was very excited. However, he was destined not to became an MP, for he was defeated at the polls.

Florence As A Young Lady

There were many more important matters in life than becoming an MP as far as the Nightingales were concerned and it did not take them long to overcome their disappointment. One of these matters concerned their daughters. Both, now aged seventeen and eighteen respectively, had to be found suitable husbands. First however, the 'Grand Tour' of Europe had to be undertaken.

The Grand Tour

For nearly three years, the family, accompanied by servants and travelling in a specially converted carriage, toured major European cities. They took the oppportunity of their absence abroad to enlarge their house at Elmsley Park.

For the two young ladies, all the languages, the literature of Greece, Rome, Egypt and France that they had learnt came to life at last. For Florence, London and the rest of England were dull in comparison with her place of birth in Italy. This slightly built young lady with chestnut brown hair was swept up into an 'Arabian Nights' Dream' come true as she danced into the small hours of the morning in the capitals of Europe.

During the day, the splendour of the cathedrals and art galleries they visited combined to add a dreamlike quality to everything around her. However, the 'dream' was sometimes shattered. Many parts of Europe had been devastated by years of war. The countryside took the brunt of the damage and the poor like those in England, lived 'squalid lives'. Florence, observant as ever, took careful notes in her diary of everything she saw.

In Geneva, Switzerland, there were many political refugees who had escaped from their own war-torn countries. Austria still occupied parts of Italy and Germany and those fighting for Home Rule had to flee for fear of being killed. Florence shared many of their dreams and hopes, and envied the fact that in contrast to her own life, there was a purpose to theirs.

CHAPTER 4

FLORENCE RETURNS TO ENGLAND

Florence Begins To Care For The Sick

On her return to England, and much to the disapproval of her parents, Florence helped care for the sick in surrounding villages who were victims of the outbreak of the dreaded scarlet fever epidemic of 1805. She wrote, 'My mind is absorbed with the idea of the sufferings of man ... I can hardly see anything else. All the people I see are eaten up with care or poverty or disease.'

At the age of twenty-five, Florence had already seen enough of the dreadful living conditions of the poor to convince her of the cause to which she would dedicate the rest of her life.

However, Florence was not only moved by the plight of the poor, but also by the more exciting world of science which was now opening up. She was one of the few women who attended a lecture given by Michael Faraday on his new discovery, electricity, which would soon replace gas lights in homes, streets and work places all over England and later, the rest of the world.

Despite her work among the poor and sick, Florence, at the age of twenty-six, was still not permitted by her parents to walk alone on the streets of London. It was not safe enough for her to do so and of course, wealthy young ladies did not go out without being accompanied by an older relative or by a maid.

It was to take her six more years until she was thirty-two, to receive her parents' consent to follow her chosen career – nursing. In truth, such a decision was not made only by her parents; aunts and uncles had to be consulted as well. This was because of the close family ties which existed. Also, nursing was a very new vocation and had not yet become the caring profession it is today, and those members of the family who were against her becoming a nurse had to be won over.

Florence Trains As A Nurse

Eventually, and to her relief, the family agreed that she could train as a nurse. But, in order to hide the fact from those who were still against the idea, her mother and sister accompanied her as though they were all going on holiday. Her mother described her as 'a wild swan hatched into a family of ducks'.

Kaiserwerth

It was while 'on holiday' that Florence was permitted to spend three months in a hospital in Kaiserwerth, Germany, run by the village pastor, 'to encourage young Christian women to care for the poor'.

Conditions at Kaiserwerth where she spent three months, were every spartan and simple. The clothes, food and living accommodation were extremely basic, but she was at peace with her surroundings. After her training, she took the opportunity to visit other similar institutions in Paris.

Full-Time Job As A Nurse

On her return to England, she was bursting with new ideas and very anxious to put them into practice. But, she faced another uphill task - how to persuade her family to agree for her to work? Women of her class did not work and especially not as nurses! When Florence suggested that she would like to work at the Salisbury Infirmary, her mother became hysterical and could think of nothing else but the disgrace her daughter would bring to the family by tending to the sick and poor.

Part of the reason for Mrs Nightingale's unhappiness at Florence's desire to work, was that in those days, hospitals were not just where the poor were sent when ill, but they were not expected to come out alive. The rich nursed their sick relatives at home. Gradually it began to dawn on Florence that the time had come when she could no longer expect any support from her family. She had to become more assertive.

Eventually her family could do nothing to stop Florence from doing what was clearly her choice and some might say, her 'calling'. She obtained a position as a supervisor at a sanitarium for 'Sick Gentlewomen and Governesses' at 1 Harley Street, London. She was not expected to do any actual nursing and was not to be paid for her services. The job was purely voluntary, but at least she would be able to do the type of work she had always wanted. In the end, her father relented and provided her with an income of £500 per year with which to rent rooms and to live.

The sanitarium at 1 Harley street proved to be a challenge to Florence as many of the new ideas she wanted to introduce had to be approved by the governing body and the rest of the staff.

Florence saw that many changes were needed such as fresh air and proper ventilation in the wards, regular changes of bed linen and the daily bathing of patients. Also, all animals had to be banned from the wards and a balanced diet was to be prepared in clean kitchens so that the sick would recover better. Of no less importance and concern to her was the sanitataion around the hospital. This was very basic and had to be improved. Last but by no means least, the staff caring for the patients had to be trained.

Florence was well on her way towards achieving most of these objectives when the war in the Crimea intervened.

CHAPTER 5

FLORENCE GOES TO THE CRIMEA

The Crimean War

Although Britain is now on friendly terms with the rest of the countries in Europe, this has not always been the case. For three years from 1853 to 1856, France, Turkey and Britain fought against Russia. Most of the fighting took place around the port of Sebastopol in the Black Sea and the war was called the 'Crimean War'.

From the start, the war was a fiasco. Hundreds of men lost their lives. Many died not so much from their wounds, but from the diseases which they caught because of the lack of medical and nursing care, clothing that was unsuitable for the climate they were fighting in and poor organisation.

The Public Demands Medical Care For Soliders At The Front

When news of the fighting and the many casualties was made public by the new improved telegraph system, people in England were very angry. *The Times* newspaperd helped publicise the awful conditions further in reports sent back by their war correspondent, W.H. Russell, and asked in large headlines, **WHY HAVE**

WE NO SISTERS OF MERCY TO TAKE CARE OF THE WOUNDED AND SICK? This stirred the government into taking action, and Sidney Herbert, Secretary of War, invited Florence to organise a body of nurses and to go to Scutari in Turkey. In the meantime, a Nightingale Fund was set up to help finance the nurses' work from public donations.

At last the moment Florence had been waiting for all her life had come. Now she felt she could really be of help to the sick and serve her country as well. She was appointed supervisor of a team of thirty-eight women recruited to nurse the sick and injured. The women were from a mixed background and only a few had previous nursing experience. This was the first time the British government had recruited women to care for those wounded on the battlefield.

It was to be expected that Florence Nightingale and her band of nurses would meet with the utmost of objections. They were entering a man's world. The few women who were anywhere around were the wives of officers and those who followed the forces and sold food and other goods – they were called 'sutlers'. Both the medical staff and the commanding officers regarded Florence and the other nurses as nuisances wasting the army's time at the front. On top of all this hostility Florence also had to face the wasteful routine of filling in requisition forms – a procedure which was adhered to regardless of the number of casualties.

The Barrack Hospital at Scutari was no different from hospitals at home, and, to make matters worse, it had been built over a refuse dump. It was simply too small to cope with the increase in numbers requiring medical attention. However, Florence was very careful not to tread on the toes of the medical staff by being too critical or forceful.

It was only when a violent storm, combined with the bitter winter conditions, led to a virtual collapse in the official hospital administration that it was possible for her and the nurses to play a more active role in reorganising the hospital and providing better conditions for the sick and wounded.

Florence Travels To The Front

When time permitted and after all her chores at the hospital were finished, she would ride to the front to care for the men there and to see for herself how she could help them.

The very presence of women nurses on the battlefield was a great comfort to the soldiers who previously had only been used to the rough and ready treatment they received at the hands of the army's medical officers. Florence and her nurses brought a more gentle approach to the way in which these sick soldiers were cared for.

When Florence saw how brave the men were and what sacrifices they went through for their country, her respect for them grew in leaps and bounds. The men became aware that while their officers continued to beat them and generally treat them like the scum of the earth, here was Miss Nightingale, a member of a wealthy family, treating them with care and respect. Indeed both nurses and soldiers came from what was termed the 'dregs of society'. Both however emerged as heroes and heroines of the war whilst the officers, generals and administrators who were more often chosen because of their wealth and class received nothing but criticism because of the way they had conducted the war. The long hours she worked, her neglect of her own health, and the lack of proper food whilst she was in the Crimea gradually took their toll on Florence. She herself took ill and had to to be nursed back to good health.

Fighting In The Crimea

CHAPTER 6

THE LADY WITH THE LAMP'S LEGEND SPREADS IN ENGLAND

The Lady With The Lamp

After the war was over, the soldiers returned home to their families and spread the good news of the work done for them by Miss Nightingale and her nurses. The soldiers' return also marked the beginning of a legend popularised in songs, poetry and personal memories, by those who had been at the front. The most popular image that those songs and rhymes gave rise to was that of the 'lady with the lamp', bending over wounded soldiers, treating them and saying kind and gentle words.

Scores of baby girls born during this time were named Florence after her. The souvenir industry which had prospered after the wedding of Queen Victoria and Prince Albert, rose to the new occasion and produced an assortment of maps, plates and mugs celebrating her good work.

Florence Establishes Hospitals

However, there was to be another phase in Miss Nightingale's career. After the war, tired and exhausted, she made her way back to the family's home, ignoring the official plans made to welcome her back.

She was now a private person again, sick and in need of rest after nearly two years of what must have been pure hell in the Crimea. One of the first people she went to see was Queen Victoria who wanted to hear a first-hand account of what the war had been like.

Once recovered, she went on to live for another forty years, all of which were dedicated to improving the conditions under which sick civilians, soldiers and nurses were cared for. She had begun to think about this soon after her recovery. For one thing, she had enormous public support and although she was not a member of parliament or a civil servant, she had many friends in high places. Florence realised she would face many barriers in her fight to change conditions in hospitals, but she was still determined to use what inlfuence she could to bring these changes about.

Most of the new laws affecting the training of nurses and the conditions of hospital buildings and general sanitation which were passed during the latter half of the nineteenth century both in England and overseas were as a result of Florence Nightingale's influence.

Training School For Nurses Established

The money raised to support the Nightingale Fund was later used to set up a training school for nurses. The school was attached to the new St. Thomas's hospital in Waterloo. In time the experiences gained by that hospital in having trained nurses and later, trained midwives, spread to many other parts of the world.

Florence In Old Age

There were many changes in government in the last years of Florence's life. It could be said that her work was the one stable factor among all the upheavals of the late nineteenth century. Florence was consulted by many government ministers and civil servants both from Britain and abroad. In a sense, 'she held court', whether it was on hospital design and administration, drainage, ventilation, hygiene, diet or the training of nurses.

Florence lived to be ten years short of a century and was never tired of working. Despite her own ill health she was able to care for many of her loved ones including her sister, Parthenope, her mother, Fanny and her father.

Towards the end of her life, she began to lose her sight and was cheered by the presence of her many nieces, nephews and cousins who came to visit her and read to her.

Before her death on August 13 1910, she had requested that only a small cross should mark her grave. Her final wish was that her inheritance should be used to build a barracks with day rooms and sports facilities for soldiers.

Her legacy to people the world over was her overwhelming care and concern for the poor everywhere.

MARY SEACOLE – 'DOCTRESS'

Mary As A Young Girl

CHAPTER 1

BIRTH

'I was born a Creole in the town of Kingston on the island of Jamaica, sometime in the present century and have good Scottish blood coursing in my veins', wrote Mary Jane Seacole – 'Mother Seacole', 'Doctress' in her autobiography.

She does not mention the year or date of her birth. Such details are either unknown or were not considered important. What is known however is that she was born in 1805, the year in which the Battle of Trafalgar was being fought off the coast of Spain. She was born in a century which has seen the most important changes in modern history.

Mary was proud of both her African and Scottish ancestry. Her mother was an African Doctress and Inn Keeper. Her father was an officer in one of the Scottish regiments stationed on the island. Mary's immediate family consisted of Edward, her brother, Louisa, her sister and her mother's mother as well as many pets.

CHAPTER 2

JAMAICA

Some of the richest islands in the world are set in the Caribbean sea. Britain, France, Spain and Holland found it necessary to keep parts of their navies and armies in the region and the islands which they captured were called colonies. Each of these countries' ships were often raided by pirates and their cargoes of gold and other valuables stolen. The most notorious pirates were 'Edward Teach', 'Black Beard' and 'Calico Jack'.

Xaymaca, meaning land of many springs was the Arawak spelling of Jamaica. The Arawaks were the original inhabitants of the island and the word, 'tobacco' comes from the name of the pipes Christopher Columbus saw them smoking when he landed there. There are no Arawaks alive on the island today; they were all killed by the cruelty of the early Spanish invaders or died of diseases spread by the newcomers who had built plantations for growing sugar and other produce. So, workers had to be found from elsewhere to till the fields and carry out other tasks. No nationality was spared in the search for more workers.

Refugees From The Thirty Years' War

There were many people escaping the Thirty Years' War (a long war that lasted from 1618 to 1648 and was fought between Austria, Denmark, France, Holland, Germany, Spain and Sweden and which destroyed central Europe, especially large areas of Germany).

Hundreds of Irish and Scots who had been taken prisoner by Oliver Cromwell's army after the execution of Charles I in England, thousands of men and women running away from persecution because of their religious beliefs and also people who had been put in prison for committing crimes like stealing sheep; all these people were encouraged to go and settle in the West Indies.

Kidnapping

When the colonisers could not get enough of these types of people to go to Jamaica and other West Indian islands, they started to kidnap them off the streets of cities like London and Liverpool and take them on board ships bound first for Africa and then for the West Indies.

Beginning Of The African Slave Trade

The reason the ships went to Africa was so they could pick up Africans who had also been kidnapped, although sometimes they were sold to be transported to the West Indies as slaves. The colonisers had found that even with all the people from Europe whom they had encouraged to settle on the islands, they still did not have enough to supply all the labour they needed. So, they turned their attention to getting people from Africa.

Although most of the Europeans who went to the islands were forced to work without wages – they were known as 'indentured labourers' – they were usually given their freedom after a set number of years. This was not the case with the Africans who had no set time to the number of years which they had to work.

Workers, soldiers and sailors were not the only 'imports' to the islands; almost everything else that was required on the island, from food and clothing to machinery, was brought in from Europe, Africa and the Americas.

CHAPTER 3
MARY'S PARENTS

Mary's Parents

Jamaica was a British colony and Mary's father, Mr. Grant, was an officer stationed there with perhaps the 96th Regiment of the British Army. The regiment was based in Kingston which had been founded after the original garrison town and capital of the island, Port Royal, had been all but destroyed by the hurricane of 1692.

In time Kingston became a very important garrison town similar to Dover. Ships called at the port to be repaired, obtain fresh fruit, vegetables and water and to trade. Many soldiers and sailors who were ill or injured rested and obtained treatment in Kingston. The town soon became home to two barracks for British soldiers, one at Up Park and the other at New Castle.

Mary's mother, Mrs Grant, was one of the people who had been taken from Africa. As time passed, it was possible for some Africans to buy their freedom or to be granted it by the owners of the plantations on which they worked.

Many African women were able to keep small vegetable gardens from which they could feed their families and sell any surplus vegetables. The money earned and saved in this way was used to purchase their freedom. Mrs Grant worked hard on her vegetable garden and once free, she worked even harder and made a lot of sacrifices so that she could become an inn keeper and buy her own inn, Blundell Hall, in Kingston.

Mrs Grant set up Blundell Hall as a home for officers and their wives who were ill or injured or just in need of good company and home cooking. She used her knowledge of herbal medicines to treat those who were sick.

Mrs Grant was not only a good cook, but she remembered many of the herbal treatments she had been taught by her mother and used them to cure the sick. Medicines, chemists and hospitals as we know them today did not exist. She was not the only African 'doctress' on the island. There were many others like her. Women such as Couba Cornwallis who attended Admiral Horatio Nelson as well as Prince William who later became King William IV were all known as 'doctresses'.

CHAPTER 4

EARLY CHILDHOOD

Blundell Hall

Blundell Hall was one of the landmarks in Kingston. It was situated on East Street, not very far away from the Parade. The Parade consisted of barracks, a court house, a theatre and a church, all built to form a square.

Growing Up In Kingston

Mary's childhood was very happy. It is difficult to picture exactly what it was like, but, in the story of her life written when she was in her fifties she says, 'When I was a young child I was taken by an old lady who brought me up in her household among her own grandchildren and who could scarcely show me more kindness had I been one of them.' She goes on to say '... indeed, I was so spoiled by my kind patroness that for being frequently with my mother, I might very likely have grown up idle and useless.'

Mary grew up amidst the smells, sounds and bustle of the Parade. She was awoken not only by the church bells, but also by the army bugle sounding the reveille. The fife and drums of the soldiers dressed in their bright uniforms added colour to the young girl's life. Through the flaps of the jalousied windows of Blundell Hall, she would catch glimpses of the visitors arriving in their carriages.

It appears that as in many parts of Africa, children would be cared for by older women within their communal compound. A similar pattern of care had taken root in Jamaica and still exists today. This custom helped relieve Mary's mother of the task of caring for Mary especially during busy periods of house building, the arrival of numerous ships in the harbour or the outbreak of a sickness which required all of Mrs Grant's attention as a doctress.

Mary described the woman who took care of her as

Blundell Hall

an 'old lady'. She was therefore not her grandmother or indeed a relative of any kind. But this made no difference to the love and care she received. As any child who grew up in the West Indies and was cared for by their grandmother will tell you, it was the best period of their lives.

Indeed, Mary shared the love of both her mother and her adopted mother who lived nearby. She was forever grateful for this and cared for both of them in their old age when they were no longer able to do so for themselves. This love which she received in abundance helped her in her turn to show much love to others.

Kingston Market

Sundays were not only a time for church but also for Mary and her mother to visit the Sunday market. It was the one day of the week when most people were free. The market stalls would be piled high with vegetables such as yams, eddoes and sweet potatoes. Guavas, golden apples, sour sop, bananas, mangos and many other fruits would glisten in the sun. Pigs, goats and fowl were all displayed for sale. Many women spent what little spare time they had making baskets, mats, jams, pepper and other sauces all for sale at the market.

Once the hustle and bustle of the market was over, Mary may have been taken to the theatre to see the tightrope act of Monsieur Du Mulin. One of the most daring of his acts was performed with children strapped to his feet, not the sort of act which would be permitted today.

Mary Learns Her Mother's Skills

It is doubtful whether Mary attended school, so she would have had more than enough time to observe, to think and to do all the other things children do. What Mary missed by not attending formal school was certainly made up for as she accompanied her mother on her daily routine.

In addition to the usual household chores which she was given to do, she was expected to collect payment for the services and goods sold at the inn and to learn at first hand the names and uses of the various herbs grown by her mother for use in making her medicines. However, it was never a case of all work and no play for

The Kitchen At Blundell Hall

Mary. In no time at all, she was not content just to watch her mother at work, and when tired of the company of grown-ups, she had other interests. She spent hours giving first aid to her pets, whether they required it or not. On most days, her cats, dogs and other pets could be seen with bandages and splints healing imaginary wounds. The poor creatures were also given herbal medicine with careful note being taken by Mary of their reactions to the potions she had given them.

Travellers' Tales

Although amusements were few, they were noisy and happy affairs. The John Canoe Band which played and danced in the streets during the Christmas holidays was a favourite of young and old alike. Mary was often entertained by the guests at Blundell Hall. Her name was a constant reminder of their own childhood to those guests who came from England and they would recite the rhymes they had learnt then. The most popular one was:

> 'Mistress Mary, quite contrary
> How does your garden grow?
> With silver bells
> And cockle shells
> And pretty maids all in a row'

Other popular and well-known tunes of the day soon became as familiar to her as they were to children in England.

Mary's imagination was fired by the stories these visitors told of faraway lands, of soldiers, of battles, of Calico Jack, the pirate, of hidden treasure, of King Bruce of Scotland and the spider and the leprechauns in Ireland. She was told of the bravery of the Africans who had fought for and won their freedom and now lived in Cockpit Country in Jamaica as well as stories about Ananse. No wonder the urge to travel grew so strong in her as she sat tracing her fingers along the well-worn map of the world which her mother kept.

There was of course, another side to Kingston which Mary could not have missed since East Street was not far from the Parade. The court house on the Parade would have been the scene for many a trial of Africans who refused to work for no wages. Some pretended to be ill, many ran away and when attempts were made to capture and bring them back they fought for their freedom. Mary would have seen the preparations being made for the soldiers to break the Africans' strike. The rebellion of 1831 led by Samuel Sharpe would not have gone unnoticed by Mary as troops rode out of Kingston to put down the rebellion. The punishment for going on strike was public flogging and hanging.

CHAPTER 5

MARY SETS OFF FOR ENGLAND

At long last when she was twelve years old, Mary's mother decided that the time had come for her daughter to visit England. Blundell Hall hummed with activity and excitement as preparations were made for the journey.

It seemed that every visitor had advice to give her of places she should see and the people she should visit. Warm clothes were sewn for her. Although there was no need for her to have a passport as we know it today, she would have had to carry travel documents with her. It was to have been her first trip by sea, the first time she had left the island and her first time away from home.

Mary Arrives in England

Bristol docks where Mary first landed in England were abuzz with scores of sailing ships. The climate in England was so different to that of sunny Jamaica that it seemed to put a greater distance between her and her home. The fog, dampness and smoking chimneys on all the roofs gave every home the appearance of a factory. The year was 1817 - eight years before the first railway was built - and Mary's journey to London would have been by coach.

The slowness of the journey to London added to her excitement and she was able to take in the scenery of the surrounding countryside as the coach travelled towards London. They passed gardens, castles, country mansions of the rich and miners' and agricultural workers' cottages. The long wars which England had fought against the French had ended, and the people they met on the way were less worried about battles with the French than they would have been a few years earlier.

Mary Arrives In London

On arriving in London her excitement knew no bounds. The sights and sounds she saw and heard were beyond her wildest dreams. The large buildings, fountains, statues, wide streets, the shops and historical buildings like Buckingham Palace, brought to life all the stories that she had been told about England.

However, there was another side to London, a fear and dislike of people who looked different to Londoners and who chose to worship in a different church. Walking along the streets of London, Mary was exposed to unpleasant remarks about the colour of her skin. She was called names by children who were about the same age as herself but she did not lash out or reply in kind.

As a child growing up in Jamaica Mary does not mention having been taunted because of her colour. There were over 60,000 Creoles or more than twice the white population in Jamaica. Mary in later life spoke very highly of the hard work and skill of other Creoles and especially of the women who were owners of inns, herbal doctors, traders, seamstresses and milliners.

Sometimes people are prejudged because of their skin. On other occasions, the words 'coloured' or 'half-caste' may be used to express disgust for no reason other than to hurt a person of mixed race.

Because she was full of confidence, love and compassion when faced by these taunts on the streets of London, one could almost say that the rhyme, 'Sticks and stones may break my bones, but harsh words will never hurt me', was written by her.

While still in London, Mary was able to meet some of her father's relatives. With this picture of her parental ancestry complete, she was able to set sail for Jamaica, after spending almost a year in England, with even more self-confidence and lots of new ideas and adventures to share with her family and friends back home. She was to return to England several times during the coming years.

CHAPTER 6

MARY RETURNS TO JAMAICA

Mary Becomes Her Mother's Apprentice

Once she was back in Jamaica, life at Blundell Hall was very much as it had been before she left except that now Mary was the one with tales of faraway places to tell. The guests at the Hall were obliged to listen to her instead of her being the listener.

In the autumn of 1818 not very long after her return from England, Jamaica was struck by two hurricanes which caused much damage and loss of life.

By now, Mary was more like a companion to her mother. She took a greater interest in Blundell Hall. There was of course, much to do. The kitchen was the hub of all the activities. Jams and beverages had to be prepared and, depending on which fruits were in season, they used them to make these preserves. Guavas, plums, pineapples and mangos bought from the Sunday market or grown in their own garden would all be piled up on the kitchen table ready for slicing, boiling and bottling.

Mary and her mother gathered spices like pimento, cloves, nutmeg and allspice. The different herbs such as bay leaves, lemon grass and roots, vines and berries from which they made their medicines and mixtures were either picked from their garden or from the surrounding countryside.

Mary's mother was of course, an excellent cook. The savoury aromas of Irish stew and Scotch broth mingled with those of ackee, cod fish, fried chicken and rice and peas, no doubt making it difficult for Blundell Hall's guests to decide quite what to order for their meals!

Mary was very fortunate. Life had been good to her. Many on the island were still not free to earn wages or to travel and it was not until 1838 that they became free. Others who were able to buy their freedom, travelled to other islands in search of work.

Mary Visits Other Caribbean Islands

While still in her twenties, Mary paid her first visit to Haiti, Cuba and the Bahamas and other countries in the region. Travelling in those days was very rough-going and it took a brave woman to put up with all the discomfort and dangers.

On one occasion while on a visit to Honduras, the ship in which Mary was travelling caught fire and she nearly lost her life as well as all her possessions. To pay for her travel expenses, Mary made jams and pickles which she sold in Kingston. When she was abroad she was always on the look-out for new medicines and collected many herbs which were unknown in Jamaica.

CHAPTER 7

MARY'S WORK IN JAMAICA

The year is 1838. Mary is aged eighteen. She had travelled to many countries and is now a 'doctress' in her own right. In fact, she has become a well-known Kingston personality. Her mother is getting on in years and her brother has left for Panama to work. It is time for her to think of her own personal future.

Marriage To Mr. Seacole

In 1836 she married Edwin Horatio Seacole. This was a very happy marrige but it did not last long. Mary was both wife and nurse to her husband but he died very soon after they were married. Her mother also died quite soon after her husband. The loss of the two people she loved most kept her in a state of depression for some time. She did not remarry.

However, such setbacks were not to deter her from what seemed to have become her mission in life – caring for the sick. Not even the loss of all her possessions when her house burnt down in 1843 put her off her goal. So long as there were people needing care and attention, she had enough to do to take her mind off her own misfortunes.

Discovery Of A Cure For Yellow Fever

During the next few years, her skill and experience were much in demand as serious outbreaks of yellow fever and cholera took place both in Jamaica and Panama. Mary worked alongside European doctors with whom she shared her experience and knowledge and her work was constantly being drawn to the attention of both the civilian and military authorities on the island.

By this time, Mary had performed her first examination of a dead person – a *post mortem* – to find out the reason for the person's death. She had also developed a medicine which had cured yellow fever and cholera and which was put to good use in Panama in 1850 when there was a yellow fever epidemic there.

She had now become so well-known that she was put in charge of all the medical staff on the island when yellow fever broke out there in 1853. It must be remembered that a hundred years ago diseases such as cholera, yellow fever and dysentry caused the deaths of thousands of people and were taken very seriously because they spread quickly from country to country.

Mary was very content. Her work among the sick in Jamaica was going well. But, there was worrying news from Europe of a war in which Britain was involved.

Mary In Her Forties

CHAPTER 8

MARY SEACOLE RETURNS TO ENGLAND

News of the fighting in the Crimea soon spread to Jamaica and Mary's concern grew when she learnt that men belonging to some of the regiments that had served in Jamaica were taking part in the war. The lack of adequate care and attention for the injured, many of whom were her personal friends, finally made her decide to travel once again to England.

From the outset, Mary realised that although her work was very well-known in the West Indies and in Central America, this would not be the case in England. So, before setting out, she obtained letters from all the important poeple whom she had treated and who knew about her work.

Mary Volunteers For The Crimea

When newspapers called for volunteers to serve in the war, she answered the call by presenting her letters to the War Office and other government departments in London. However, she was turned down wherever she went even though she was perhaps the most experienced person in England at that time and probably the only one capable of treating the war-wounded in the Crimea. Her first reaction to the refusals to use her skills was to have a good cry. She was angry because most of the nurses recruited had no experience. She wondered whether it was because of the colour of her skin.

While she was working in Panama, she had experienced racism from white people there who came from the southern states of America. She was shocked and disappointed, but because of her self-confidence she did not spend too much time worrying about the reasons for the refusals. Instead, she set about planning to make the journey to the Crimea independently. Clearly, she was not to be put off from what she considered to be her destiny.

Preparations For The Journey To The Crimea.

Her main problem however was how to finance the trip. Eventually, she found a business partner, a Mr. Day. The idea was to set up a company which was to provide hot meals and medical care and all necessary comforts for the troops at the front – no expense was to be spared. Today, all this would be provided for the army by the government. In the 1850s, this was not the case and people like Mary Seacole were left to fill the gap.

At last all the preparations were complete. Medical supplies of all descriptions including medicines she had brought with her from Jamaica; hams, cheeses, tea, sugar, everything she could think of from, as she said, 'an anchor to a needle' was gathered together ready for the journey. She recruited some other people, and together they set sail on the steamship *Hollander* for a journey of two to three thousand miles. It was a very cold grey morning in January 1855 when the *Hollander* left taking Mary and her companions on their historic journey to the Crimea. They arrived at Sebastopol in the summer of that year.

CHAPTER 9

IN THE CRIMEA

The 'British Hotel'

On her way to the battle front, she met Florence Nightingale and her party of nurses at Scutari. As far as Mary was concerned however, Scutari was too far away from the actual fighting and she continued on her journey so she could be nearer the front.

After a journey of several months, Mary and her party set up shop in a house near Sebstopol; she called it the 'British Hotel'. From the start, her services became legendary. With total disregard for her own health and safety, she went among the wounded with hot cups of tea, medicines, bandages and consoling words. Many of the wounded preferred to be treated by her rather than by the doctors provided by the army. Those who had known her in Jamaica could not believe their eyes; it was 'Mother Seacole', the 'Doctress' come to tend their wounds. Her very presence there often speeded their recovery.

The winter of 1856 was very severe and the men were ill-prepared for the cold. The summer of the following year brought with it many tropical illnesses about which Mary had much knowledge and experience. Whatever the need was, Mary was always at hand to be of help. All who were in need of her help received it whether they were the Turks, British or French.

At times things were very difficult. Many of the goods she had brought with her were either lost or stolen. Despite all the setbacks Mary loved the thrill and excitement of being at the front. She even took bets that when the city of Sebastopol was captured she would be the first woman to enter it. Finally the city was captured and the war suddenly came to an end, but, not before her services came to the attention of W.H. Russell, the war correspondent of *The Times*, who paid tribute to her good work:

'She is always in attendance on the battlefields to aid the wounded ... I have seen her go down under five with her little store of creature comforts for our wounded men and a more skilful hand about a wound or a broken limb could not be found among our best surgeons.

I have witnessed her devotion and her courage; I have already borne testimony to her service to all who needed them ... and I trust that England will not forget the one who nursed her sick and who sought out her wounded to aid and succour them and who performed the last office for some of her illustrious dead.'

It was now time for Mary Seacole to bid goodbye to friends and comrades, many of whom she had met for the first time and who might at first have been a bit doubtful of her abilities but who were soon won over by her kindness and devotion to their well-being.

The Wonderful Adventures
Of Mary Seacole

Arriving back in England, Mary set about rebuilding her life. First the company which was set up by Mr. Day and herself had to be wound up. What was she to do? It soon occurred to her that an account of her experiences in the Crimea, Jamaica and other Caribbean islands would be of sufficient interest to the public. Many other people were doing the same thing, so why should she not do so?

Within a year the book, *Wonderful Adventures of Mary Seacole in Many Lands*, was in the shops and proved very successful. In the meantime Mary's many friends who had been aware of her selfless contribution started raising money for her. Funds were raised at concerts as well as from public donations. Queen Victoria together with many of the leading soldiers and dignitaries of the day, lent their support to the cause. For her heroism, she received the Crimea Medal from the British government, the Legion d'Honneur from the French and the Order of the Mejidie from the Turks.

In 1856 *Punch* magazine published this tribute to her.

TRIBUTE TO MARY SEACOLE

No store she set upon epaulette
be it worsted or gold lace;
for KCB or plain private Smith
She had still one pleasant face.

And not alone was her kindness shown
To the hale and hungry lot
Who drank her grog, and ate her prog,
And paid her honest shot.

The sick and sorry can tell the story
Of her nursing and dosing deeds;
Regimental MD never worked as she,
In helping sick men's needs.

Of such work, God knows, was as much as
    she chose
That dreary winter-tide
When death hung o'er the damp and
    pestilent camp
And his scythe swung far and wide.

She gave her aid to all who prayed
To hungry, sick and cold,
Open hands and heart alike ready to part
Kind words and acts and gold.

And be the right man in the right place
    who can
The right woman was Dame Seacole.

CHAPTER 10

MARY IN OLD AGE

Mary's Last Years

The remaining days of Mary Seacole's life were spent between Jamaica and London. That she lived to the ripe old age of seventy-six despite all the dangers she had undertaken is a tribute to her fighting spirit. Other qualities which she had and which also stood out were her independence, especially at a time when the majority of women were not permitted to work, and her caring personality as well as her good business sense.

Mrs Seacole, as was to be expected, was possibly trading in preserves, herbs and medicines as before; that is when she was not travelling. Her skills it appears did not only extend to curing fevers and healing wounds, but also included massage. When the Prince of Wales was suffering from lameness in his leg, it was Mary Seacole who attended him.

On May 1 1881, the heroine of the Crimea died at 3 Cambridge Street, Paddington in west London. At the time of her death her estate was valued at £2,615.11 shillings and 7 pence. At today's prices, this may not seem much, but, a century ago, it would have been worth many thousands of pounds. At least Mary did not die in poverty.

In her will, some of the money and other property were left to her sister Louisa, other relatives and some public figures who had come to her aid in less well-off times.

Although the Crimea Campaign was a short period in her long life, it was her most important and this is what she had to say about what it meant to her:

'Let me, in a few words as possible, state the results of of my Crimean campaign. To be sure, I returned from it shaken in health. I came home wounded, as many others did. Few constitutions, indeed, were the better for those winters before Sebastopol, and I was too hard worked not to feel their effects; for a little labour fatigues me now – I cannot watch my sickbeds as I could – a week's want of rest quite knocks me up now. Then I returned bankrupt in fortune. Whereas others in my position may have come back to England rich and prosperous, I found myself poor – beggared. So few words can tell what I have lost.

But what have I gained? I should need a volume to describe that fairly; so much is it, and so cheaply purchased by suffering ten times worse than what I have experienced. I have more than once heard people say that they would gladly suffer illness to enjoy the delights of convalescence, and so, by enduring a few days' pain, gain the tender love of relatives and sympathy of friends. And on this principle I rejoice in the trials which have borne me such pleasures as those I now enjoy, for wherever I can go I am sure to meet some smiling face; every step I take in the crowded London streets may bring me in contact with some friend, forgotten by me, perhaps, but who soon reminds me of our old life before Sebastopol; it seems very long ago now, when I was of use to him and he to me.

Where indeed, do I not find friends? In omnibuses, in river steamboats, in places of public amusement, in quiet streets and courts, where taking short cuts I lose my way oft-times, spring up old familiar faces to remind me of the months spent on Spring Hill. The sentries at Whitehall relax from the discharge of their important duty of guarding nothing to give me a smile of recognition; the very newspaper offices look friendly as I pass them by; busy Printing-house Yard puts on a cheering smile, and the *Punch* office in Fleet Street sometimes laughs outright. Now, would all this have happened if I had returned to England a rich woman? Surely not.'

The Friends of Mary Seacole

Although during the Crimea War Mary Seacole's name was linked to Florence Nightingale's, and both were regarded as heroines, her name simply disappeared from the history books for well over a century. It was not until 1981 when nurses from the West Indies and Africa rediscovered her work, that her name became well-known once more. With the help of others these nurses formed the Friends of Mary Seacole, an organisation which is dedicated to restoring her name to its rightful place as one of the world's greatest women.

To this end, the Friends of Mary Seacole laid a new headstone on Mary's grave at Kensal Rise Cemetery in North London.

POSTSCRIPT

Common Bonds Between Two Pioneers

It would perhaps be very surprising if the two heroines of the Crimea had not met each other. They did in fact do so, twice. Once at the Barrack Hospital in Scutari and again at Balaclava. In her biography, Florence Nightingale records the meeting. Mary Seacole had a letter of introduction to Miss Nightingale as was the custom in those days and she describes Miss Nightingale thus:

'A . . . slight figure, in the nurses' dress: with pale, gentle hands withall firm face, resting lightly in the palm of one white hand, while the other supports the elbow – a position which gives to her countenance a keen inquiring expression, which is rather marked. Standing thus in repose, and yet keenly observant – the greatest sign of impatience at any time – a slight, perhaps unwitting motion of the firmly planted right foot – was Florence Nightingale – that English woman whose name shall never die, but sound like music on the lips of British men until the hour of doom.'

Florence Nightingale then asked Mary Seacole if there was anything she could do to help her. Mary replied that she and her companions were on their way to the front and were in need of accommodation for the night. Florence gladly provided this.

Both women have left their mark on history. Although the war in the Crimea only lasted for two years, the events that took place there were to affect the lives of millions of people the world over. Gone for ever was the need for those women who had qualified as doctors and orderlies to wear male clothing so as to disguise themselves. As a result of Florence Nightingale's and Mary Seacole's work on the battlefield, they were able to carry out their work dressed as women.

Florence and Mary had to face their share of prejudice and only overcame this through determination and the will to succeed regardless of all the odds against them. So great was their determination that no sooner had the war in the Crimea ended than both women volunteered to go to India. This was because Indian troops had mutinied against British rule. Many of the soldiers who had fought in the Crimea and were known to Miss Nightingale and Miss Seacole were to be sent to India to put down the rebellion, and they both felt that they had an obligation to those men. However, the officials at the War Office politely refused to entertain the offer.

Those same officials who had refused to accept Mrs Seacole's application to join the group of nurses which was on its way to the Crimea were at first against Florence Nightingale, and women in general entering what they regarded as a man's world – working in a military hospital.

One other common bond which linked Florence and Mary was their desire to be free. Indeed the bond stretches to include all those who were working for no wages. Some were tied physically to the owners and not permitted to exercise their freedom, while others like Florence were tied by a tradition which was as strong as any physical knot could be, to roles which they felt restricted them.

QUESTIONS DESIGNED FOR HISTORY KS3 - ATTAINMENT TARGET 1 - KNOWLEDGE AND UNDERSTANDING OF HISTORY

The Lives of Mary Seacole and Florence Nightingale

FLORENCE NIGHTINGALE

1. Which class of family was Florence born into? Give two examples of the privileges Florence and her sister enjoyed.
2. What do you understand by the expression, 'born with a silver spoon in her mouth'.
3. How did Mr. Nightingale's attitude to his daughter's education differ from that of other people in their class?
4. Briefly list the differences between the two girls. (Give three examples.)
5. List two sources of the family's wealth.
6. In the 19th century when Florence was born, many changes were taking place. List three of them.
7. Florence's family were strong liberals. How would you define this?
8. (a) What was the 'Grand Tour' and
   (b) When Florence was taken on the 'Grand Tour', what shattered her dream for her?
9. What decision did Florence come to at the age of twenty-five and why?
10. Which obstacles did she have to overcome to fulfill her destiny. List three.

11. How did the Crimean War finally change her life? Comment on:
    - the soldiers' attitude to her
    - her contribution to hygiene in the field hospitals
    - the role of female nurses
    - the wider society's attitude to cleanliness and hygiene in hospitals

MARY SEACOLE

1. What sort of a woman was Mary Seacole's mother and what was her special skill?
2. What sort of education did Mary have?
3. What skills did she learn from her mother?
4. Briefly say why Mary wanted to travel?
5. In the society of the time, Mary was the daughter of a freed African slave and a white father. What did she notice about the treatment of the black slaves?
6. When she travelled to England what did she experience which she had not experienced in Jamaica?
7. How did the death of her husband and then her mother affect her destiny?
8. For which disease did she discover a cure?
9. When Mary wanted to take her skills abroad she was unable to do so, at first. List three reasons.
10. Mary eventually found a way of travelling to the Crimean War. How?
11. Mary Seacole went straight to the battle-front. How did her special knowledge help the soldiers?
12. List three of the comments which were made about her by the soldiers she treated.

QUESTIONS FOR STRANDS 1-3

FLORENCE NIGHTINGALE

1. Using the information in the BIRTH and CHILDHOOD chapters, write between six and ten diary entries which show Florence's development from the age of about eight to sixteen. You could include:
   - Florence was very tidy, her sister was not
   - their education
   - treating 'sick' animals
   - their hobbies
   - their family etc.
2. When Florence went on her 'Grand Tour' of Europe, at the age of eighteen she saw and learnt a lot.
   Imagine that you are Florence – recalling your experiences; write an account of what you saw and how you felt after the Tour.
3. Imagine the conversation that might have taken place between Florence and her parents when she told them that she wanted to be a nurse. Write a short playscript.
4. Imagine that you are a soldier in the Crimean War, you have been wounded and have been sent to the field hospital. It is a dismal and unhealthy place until Miss Nightingale arrives. Describe her and the differences that she makes.

MARY SEACOLE

1. After reading the section 'Mary Becomes Her Mother's Apprentice' write a piece entitled 'A Day In The Life Of Mary Seacole' in which you imagine you are Mary and describe a typical day in your life.
2. Give an account of the racism she experiences in England which she did not experience in Jamaica. Say how she dealt with this racism.

3. After reading the chapter, 'Mary Volunteers For The Crimea' write a newspaper article which advertises for the volunteers.
4. Mary was given a letter of introduction to Florence Nightingale and many other influential people when she went to join the war.
   Write the letter she may have been given which introduces her to Miss Nightingale.
   - who wrote the letter
   - address
   - content: what were Mary's achievements etc.

GLOSSARY

Arawak Indians - original inhabitants of Jamaica who were exterminated by the Spanish colonists by the year 1655.

Cockpit Country - a very hilly region in the interior of Jamaica.

Faraday, Michael - generally accepted as the father of electricity.

Garrison - a supply of soldiers for guarding a fortress.

Garrison Town - a town in which a garrison is stationed.

Hovels - small, dirty, miserable dwellings.

Indentured workers - they had a written contract at the end of which they were free.

Jalousied windows - slatted blind or shutter that admits air and light but not rain.

Kingston - capital of Jamaica.

Maroons - people who refused to be enslaved and won their freedom after a long struggle.

Penny Post - a uniform system of charging a penny for an inland letter was introduced on January 10 1848. The plan was put forward by Roland Hill.